NO BIGOTRY ALLOWED:
LOSING THE SPIRIT OF FEAR

NO BIGOTRY ALLOWED:
LOSING THE SPIRIT OF FEAR

Towards the Conversation about Race

RONALD BONNER

ISBN: 1516888936
ISBN 13: 9781516888931
Library of Congress Control Number: 2015913318
CreateSpace Independent Publishing Platform
North Charleston, South Carolina

TABLE OF CONTENTS

ACKNOWLEDGMENTS

Thanks to my wife Rosetta Ross for helping me with this project, your labor of love is much appreciated. To my sons who have always made me smile by just being two great men who have made their way in the world. To my grandchildren who have helped me to see clearly the need to do more to make this a better world for future generations. To my family for their love, and to my aunts and uncles whose lives made me appreciate the struggle for justice. And to my great aunt Rebecca who just did so much to give me a narrative based on justice, love, and endurance to move forward in life, thank you, thank you all.

FOREWORD

No one wants to talk seriously about race in this country. At least, it seems that way too often. People either pretend there is no problem or suggest there is no solution. In his book, *No Bigotry Allowed: Losing the Spirit of Fear,* Ronald Bonner offers us a way into the conversation. Bonner recognizes that the race "problem" is both personal and systemic. He invites us—black, white, every color and ethnicity—to take a step back and look more objectively at the origins, history and lingering effects of racism. He begins by defining the differences and nuances of our language: race, racism, white supremacy, bigotry, and white privilege. Using an interdisciplinary approach, Bonner offers us the best thinking and practices in history, social and cultural studies, sociology, psychology, and leadership.

However, this is no mere intellectual exercise. Bonner shares from his very personal (and too often, painful) experiences and gives permission for all of us to be honest about our perceptions, perspectives, and experiences of race. He does not demonize nor judge—he gently encourages all people to be honest with each other and to listen intently to the other. Not satisfied to keep the conversation on a personal level, Ronald Bonner shows how racism, white supremacy and bigotry are embodied in the very systems of our country.

He calls for reasonable people to stand in solidarity against the powers and principalities and wickedness in our culture and society—to name the evil and work together to eliminate the vestiges of a social construct that is so destructive to all in our society. He does not shy away from taking a long look at power, privilege, and class as well as how they have been embedded in our interpersonal lives as well as our social and economic institutions and policies.

One does not have to agree with every point of Bonner's argument; this slender volume is not the last word about race. It is, however, a primer for understanding how we have gotten where we are with so much tension, misunderstanding, indifference, and hostility around race. We must begin somewhere and Bonner offers a way into the murky and difficult terrain of race—by overcoming our fear, by acknowledging our vulnerability, and by risking to trust the process that conversation will make a difference for individuals and for society. My hope is that we will take the challenge that Ronald Bonner has so eloquently laid out before us.

Barbara Essex
United Church of Christ
Cleveland, Ohio, September 2015

Barbara Essex is a minister in the United Church of Christ and the author of numerous books, including the popular *Bad Girls of the Bible: Exploring Women of Questionable Virtue*. She is currently the Executive Director of United Protestant Campus Ministries in Cleveland.

PREFACE

THE PROBLEM OF DEALING
WITH RACE IN AMERICA

The September 2012 edition of the *Harvard Business Review* included an article entitled "Are You Solving the Right Problem?" It quotes Albert Einstein who said: "If I were given one hour to save the planet, I would spend 59 minutes defining the problem and one minute resolving it."

In the United States, our racial problems are interlaced, and unless unraveled, we may spend time applying a great solution to the wrong problem. One of those problems is the conflation of racism and white supremacy as being the same thing; they are not the same thing. White supremacy is the notion, belief, or ideology that white people are innately superior to people of color. Racism is the power dynamic and construct that allows white supremacy to remain intact. White supremacy, if not for the power of racism, would have died during the period of Southern Reconstruction. Without racism, the notion of white supremacy would have been buried for good at the 1936 Olympics in Berlin. But because of the system and power of racism the notion of white supremacy is allowed to survive and thrive.

Racism keeps white supremacy alive. Racism did not end with the election of a black president, who was correct in stating that not saying the N-word in public does not denote that racism has ended. Interestingly, the media conversation following this statement by The President focused on his using the N-word, and not much attention was given to those posting negative comments about The President and their use of the N-word to attack him on his social media account.

At the heart of white supremacy and racism lies bigotry. Bigotry is more than prejudice; it is hate-filled prejudice and is the fuel that keeps the economic engine that is racism going. An example of this is the media continuing to question and reject the femininity and beauty of the Williams sisters and the natural aesthetic of black women. While Venus and Serena Williams have fought against these negative media depictions, many black girls and women still experience pain from these and other derogatory media depictions of black women.

Because so many white people rely on racism and white supremacy for their sense of self-worth, their sense of who they are, white supremacy remains alive. White supremacy remains embedded at an ontological level; it is who some people are; it is all that they have to make them feel human. And for supporting the notions of white supremacy they are rewarded with power, prestige, and privilege. Without the benefits of racism, white people would just be average people, not superior just equal. Further, white supremacy survives by the fear mongering notion that without the system of racism, white people would be treated by people of color as they have treated people of color. Thus, they fight to keep it alive and refuse to discuss issues of race while clinging to the mantra, "Black people should just get over it."

The starting point for white supremacy and racism is bigotry. When we address bigotry, a disease of the heart that is at the core of these problems, we will move the needle forward for resolving racial issues in America and the world. The book *No Bigotry Allowed: Losing the Spirit of Fear* is designed to do just that.

INTRODUCTION

In the long run, we shape our lives, and we shape ourselves. The process never ends until we die. And the choices we make are ultimately our own.

— *ELEANOR ROOSEVELT*

Bigotry is a spiritual heart disease that cuts across groups. Anyone hateful can be a bigot; all one has to do is express that hate for another person or group. Bigotry expresses hate and apathy toward others for no other reason than difference. It is bigotry that motivates white supremacy and any other form of false superiority based on a characteristic of another group. Bigotry is the force that drives the effectiveness of institutionalized bias and systemic power that creates institutionalized injustice. Once the bigotry has become institutionalized, systematic power is exercised, and the bigot can hide behind a sense of apathy, denial, or false innocence. Saying, "I am only doing my job," while knowing full well the negative impact his/her actions are having on others. To some degree, the bigot who exercises this institutionalized bias is afforded the opportunity to enjoy the harm caused to others insofar as it gives the bigot a false sense of being superior to the ones impacted.

Thus, the subject of race is still a difficult subject to approach. The subject of race continues to evoke a strong visceral reaction, whether it's "Here we go again," or "Do we have to." Many people don't like to talk about race because of the historical connection to the period of black enslavement in the Americas. The subject of race gives rise to a sense that black people need to "be over" that subject, especially in the "post-racism" era after the election of a black President of the United States. This book is designed to address the issue of bigotry, and how people of different colors or races relate to and impact one another negatively. While this book addresses issues of race, the method discussed applies to other forms of bigotry as well.

A common thought about slavery by those who don't want to discuss race issues is that it was a long time ago, and there is nothing that can be done about it now. To bring the issue of enslavement into the conversation of race often draws responses of "It happened; get over it" and "Black people should just move on." This is frequently followed by the statement, "Bad things have happened to others, and you don't see them still talking about it." The truth is other ethnic groups do talk about the injustices suffered by their ancestors. In some cases, it continues to be a source of painful memory that creates a determination and power never to let it happen again. The painful memory is present but is disguised in celebration or remembrances helping to shape their future.

The idea of a discussion about race brings up defensive postures. These defensive postures can negate the effectiveness of countermeasures like diversity training, cultural awareness, multicultural/diversity/cross-cultural training or even racial sensitivity training. These programs and efforts often miss confronting the most difficult matters of race relations. Often the presentations and group discussions are too polite and are led by persons who are careful not to offend. One persistent problem with conversations between persons of different races is the approach. When approaching the subject of racism/race as the elephant in the room, people tend to forget that this elephant built the room and the surrounding structure, missing the opportunity for an effective conversation.

A real conversation is not what most people want to have; conversations about race continue to cause back hairs to bristle. Therefore, instead of inciting meaningful conversation, we often engage in polite, intelligent, meaningless dialog. Until there is a real conversation, not much will change. Real conversation is where those involved actively make efforts to listen and understand the pain and suffering that black people still experience and the frustration that white people have come to experience. The pain that black people have experienced informs our social locations. Our counterparts have not experienced this pain and can't fully understand and appreciate our reactions, conversations and stories on how racial issues have impacted us. Real conversations must take place to remove racial divisions. Otherwise, we will continue to have a dance of engagement without real interaction, or dialogical intercourse without entanglement or understanding. In other words, we will continue just going through the motions.

This book aims to provoke and promote honest conversation. This book is an effort toward making the conversation real, by exploring the pain, creating an understanding of our different social locations, and creating a common ground or playbook for conversation between all colors of people. The hope is that this will result in moving the needle of honest conversation from denial to resolution. Often the healing process involves pain. To heal a broken bone, the bone often has to be re-broken; for some persons, surgery is often required to heal ailments; and radiation treatment with its side effects is often needed to heal cancer. Some illness requires a combination of treatments to be most effective. Racism, white supremacy, and bigotry are illnesses that plague our society and require a steady regimen of correction that is not sugar-coated or always pleasant to swallow. The result will be a real conversation and healing that can take place, employing honest dialog stripped of the myths and defenses. Real conversation is a two-way street; it will have to be a give and take.

Since the 70s, I have had real conversations about race with co-workers, friends, workshop participants, and others. The conversations I had in the early 70s have been foundational in helping me communicate with others about "race" in both formal and informal settings. These early workplace conversations were honest dialogs about race and how blacks and whites perceived one another. Our method was simple, we just – openly and honestly without displaying anger – talked. We talked about our families, and we talked about going to school, and we talked about racial issues. We talked about matters of how we were perceived by each other; we discussed likes and dislikes across racial lines. We did not hold back in what we thought or discussed, but we always engaged our conversations with respect for one another.

We had honest and frank conversations and discovered that even with our differences we had sameness; we had common desires, and we were not as bad as the stereotypes made us out to be. We were able to hear comments and accusations without getting divisive; we discovered that we could talk about anything racial, not always changing someone's opinion but recognizing that there was one. Sometimes the opinions were logical, sometimes seemingly illogical, but ontologically embedded, and we respected them regardless. Sometimes what was said was offensive, but we got through it; we often laughed at each other, sometimes with each other, and out of our efforts we grew closer as people.

Without judging, we continued to learn about each other, and we grew closer as people, not as races but as people. Without our knowing it or consciously seeking it, we were in search of common ground. Those lessons have remained with me and have allowed me to have frank and honest conversations with many people. A key element in these conversations is offering an alternative point of view to their level of comfort and distance to the concerns, helping to bridge the racial divide between neighbors and friends in waiting.

This book is not about singing "Kumbaya" or asking "Why can't we all just get along?" It is about open and frank conversation that can lead to change and creating an interpersonal, and institutional climate where "no bigotry allowed" is the new order of the day.

Chapter 1

BROKENNESS: THE SPLINTERED COMMUNITY

Racism is clearly a break in the harmony of humanity.

– RONALD BONNER

The human community or humanity is splintered, fragmented, and in some cases broken. Some people feel that as long as they have a roof over their heads, food on their tables, their right to bear arms, and a steady source of income life is grand. But as we know, a staggering number of people die each day from lack of the necessities of life. Humanity's tolerance for the suffering of others is staggering, and as long as it is not me or mine, some of us don't care. It is not my problem; too bad for them.

One can see this attitude by simply looking at responses to current events and reading the heartless comments made on social media in response to someone's misfortune. Shielded by anonymity on the internet, the base carelessness of members of our society is exacerbated. These vile statements and sentiments are all too frequent and cowardly and are directed at persons who have suffered misfortune or simply have a different opinion. Instead of seeking to understand another perspective, we expose the brokenness of our world in graphic detail and memes that are heartless reminders of humanity's incredulous inhumane treatment of one another. It appears that people are desensitized to the sufferings of other people.

One former study that points to our tolerance of the suffering of others was the Milgram Experiment that exposed how much pain a person would inflict on another by the urgings of an authority figure. Needless to say, and without going into detail, many people, with varying degrees of urging or coercing, willingly and apparently knowingly inflicted pain on an innocent person. Is it any wonder that violence and hate messages fill our news media? Is it any wonder that people are willing to hurt others for their personal benefit, or when they believe that their perceived status in life is in jeopardy?

Persons are often tolerant of the suffering of others because they are told to be so, or because they believe that there is a reward for their obedience to authority figures. Bigotry is an example where the tolerance for the suffering of others has its perceived reward of inclusion into the larger society, much like the commercial "membership has its rewards." In this way, humanity will inflict harm on an identified "other" (by race, gender, class, sexual orientation) and keep the brokenness of humanity intact.

Further, many people simply do not like to see other people doing well. Even if it is no skin off of their noses, many people do not like to see other people succeed or enjoying life. There is a sense that there is a scarcity of resources. There is this zero-sum mentality that the more someone else has the less there is for me. For some things, there is a limited amount, but the limit is often beyond measure and should not be a cause for alarm.

This zero-sum perspective has led to war. At one time, wars were started over matters of geography to obtain resources. However, over time wars eventually morphed into being started because of different ideologies, religions, or nationalities. In other words, wars often are fought because one group doesn't like another group, or they want what the other group has. Regardless of the cause of a war at some point the central purpose or goal of the war is to have control or power over another.

Since before the founding of The United States of America, the issue of race and the economics of racism served as a reason for conflict and control. For the purpose of this conversation, some people do not like and will intentionally cause harm to another human being for no other reason than the color of a person's skin. Without getting to know others, many people feel they know everything they need to know about a person with just one glance because of the color of their skin. Unfortunately, W.E.B. Dubois' statement written in 1903 is still valid, the problem of the 20th century is the color line. This is especially the case since there appears to be a reward – of inclusion in the dominant group – for oppressing people of color.

The continuing concept of modern day racism is a prime example of this system of oppression and reward. Those who oppress do so to hold onto sustained positions of power, prestige, and privilege. Racism continues to find ways to control and obstruct the equality of black people in our society. Racism is the structural or systemic power that, when applied, oppresses or denies access to the benefits of institutions based on race. Racism is not merely disliking someone of another color. Today many people confuse dislike, bias, personal discrimination, prejudice or even bigotry with racism. Racism is a social construct based on institutionalized and systemic power for the purposes of control of resources, authority and influence within our society.

Today many people-of-color, Millennials, and Gen-Xers view racism differently. They have a concept that one is racist when they don't agree with or like what their white counterparts may be doing. The fact that these young people often are told that by someone white is another example of how racism continues to find ways to control the mental advancement of and the equality of black people.

For purposes of clarity, I offer these working definitions of race and racism:

We are all members of one race which is the human race. I contend that there are different ethnic groupings of people who, due to an evolutionary process, have developed characteristics that enabled them to adapt to the geographical environments they once inhabited. Based on the climatic and biological changes over the millenniums, we have come to identify that these ethnic groups, although similar, have some observable physical differences such as skin color, hair texture, and facial features. These observable and obvious differences for economic reasons have led to a common, or conventional explanation stated as race. For purposes of this conversation, we will forgo the argument of one human race and use the term race to refer to persons who are from historically different geographical areas or continents and who as ethnic groups display historically different observable physical features.

I am using a classic definition of racism as prejudice plus power, in particular, systemic or institutional power.[1] Why do I use this definition of racism? I use it because prejudice without power is not racism. Without the power to negatively impact a group by an action a person's acts may be bigoted, hateful, mean, thoughtless, evil, but are not acts of racism. Racism is not simply a social construct about disliking individuals because of their race; it is a construct that can impact an entire group, exceptions notwithstanding, negatively because of systemic and institutionalized power.

Racism is the ability of a person of one race to negatively impact a person or group of another race at a personal, institutional, systemic, and/or cultural level because of institutional, systemic, and cultural power.

Powerless persons who are racist draw their power from close identification with white racial superiority. As an individual, one can participate in racist behavior and be a racist whenever one supports systemic racism. However,

---

1   Joseph Barndt, *Dismantling Racism: The Continuing Challenge to White America*, Minneapolis, MN: Augsburg, 1991, 28.

if one's behavior is isolated and does not have the ability to impact or harm another person, then it can be chalked up to prejudice, or bigotry, but is not actual racism. Such isolated behaviors are influenced by the racism in the culture but are not able to effectively take advantage of the systemic or institutional power of racism. There are many bigoted people in our world, some without power to cause harm and others with the power to cause harm. When the bigotry is coupled with the ability to impact negatively or harm another, racism is evident.

Racism stems from bigotry and an implied identity crisis. In his book *The Search for Common Ground*, Howard Thurman discusses the break in harmony between humanity and creation. Thurman gives several examples of how in the right context humans and other living creatures could exist peacefully, but we don't. He shares a story that crows can tell the hunter from other human beings not by the guns they carry but by the dead birds that they carry.[2] He states:

> It seems that the personal identification becomes rooted in the consciousness of every member of the flock by the timbre of the outcry... other flocks that have not themselves witnessed the murder of their kind will hear and take up the cry; and so the hunter's bad reputation may be spread through a whole region. He may change his hunting ways. Even so, generations of crows yet unborn will learn that this particular man has a crow record and must be regarded at all times as a bad risk to crow welfare.[3]

Racism is a major result of the brokenness of our world, and it creates the cries of anguish that generations of people of color have borne. It is a cry that conveys a strong message that some people have a record or a history of being a risk to people of color's welfare.

---

2 Howard Thurman, *The Search for Common Ground*, Richmond, IN: Friends United Press, 1971, 59.

3 Ibid., 59.

In Thurman's example, the crow makes a distinctive cry that has an embedded message that becomes part of the DNA that will be passed on to the unborn. It is the cry of the splintered and fragmented society; it is the cry of painful disharmony; it is the cry in response to hate and the brokenness of creation.

Humans must also cry with a distinctive sound in response to humanity's brokenness that will become part of the DNA of our society. And for the human community, we must engage in more than a simple cry of anguish, but in a cry that also reflects critical thinking and problem solving. The cry of humans should have the capacity to cause effective change by coordinated efforts that address the systemic and institutionalized forms of racism, both current and future. The cry must speak out and not be muffled as it speaks out against racist policies and systems of injustice. As it speaks, it must also educate, so unborn generations will learn how the systems of oppression operate and have worked against those who suffer from the injustices of our society.

Further, this human cry must address the human identity crisis of white supremacy, the notion that one group or ethnicity of people is innately superior to another, based on skin color. Bigotry, which gave birth to white supremacy, makes a variety of efforts to defend racism and white supremacy either intentionally or through deniability. The human cry must eliminate the false sense of superiority and entitlement based on the color of one's skin. The human cry, through a critical understanding of white supremacy and racism, must develop a pedagogy and process that successfully prepares those who seek to eradicate the racism and bigotry in our world today.

In our society, the identity crisis that Thurman speaks about is that black people are identified as less than white. This message is communicated in media images and news reports. The common usage of the word "thug" to describe young black men who have encounters with law enforcement or get excited at the end of a football game is such an example. Those instances when white men who commit crimes are described as troubled or mentality ill, but not as thugs, are further examples of this negative practice. Select words are used as a form of code to demean or devalue Black people. These words along with physical violence and other outward symbols of hate are symbolic dead crows.

Developing a pedagogy and process to address white supremacy and racism will help when a mother loses a child to violence and the perpetrator is not brought to justice. There will be more than just a distinctive cry that carries an embedded message of injustice. The cry will include a directed and controlled response that demands justice and will work to ensure it. This sense of demanding justice in the face of injustice must also become part of the DNA of the unborn in our society. It must be taught until the threat of risk from racism is eradicated.

Our task in addressing the problem of racial brokenness is to ask two questions: Does it have to remain this way? And if not, what can we do to change it?

Chapter 2

I AM AFRAID TO SPEAK BECAUSE I DON'T WANT TO BE VIEWED AS RACIST

To be yourself in a world that is constantly trying to make you something else is the greatest accomplishment.

– RALPH WALDO EMERSON

Everything that a white person says is not racist. Now sometimes, the statements and actions are racist and are designed to hinder another person based solely on their race. But at other times, race is not the issue. Sometimes the white person involved has not evolved with the times, and his remarks are not racist as much as they are just stupid. Still, we can't allow this person to continue such behavior because a hostile environment is being established which is wrong as well.

In the workplace or other formal setting, sometimes a supervisor has to counsel, correct or even discipline an employee of another color based on their performance, and it has nothing to do with issues of race or culture. An employee who is late cannot legitimately call out their supervisor for picking on them because of their color. It is not the employer's or the supervisor's responsibility to adjust work schedules because the employee is late. Now, of course, some jobs do offer flextime that may attend to issues like this (and if yours does, excellent). The point is, everything is not about race, so one should be careful before playing "*the race card.*"

Have you ever been in a situation where it feels like you were engaged in an honest and open discussion when suddenly somebody played the race card, and now you don't know what to say? *Awkward.* Anyone can play the race card. But the race card is most often viewed as a tool used by people of color to say that they are being singled out or picked on because they are black or of color.

The simple truth, not everything is about race. Sometimes a person of color is guilty of the negative behavior in question. We must remove the playing of the race card. It demeans and dumbs down the conversation regardless of who plays it. The race card, when "played" inappropriately, creates a dysfunctional response that halts positive interactions and prevents meaningful conversation or effective strategies for progress and change.

The white person who plays the race card is often a bigot, an incompetent, or the person who desires to be the group leader or savior. Most often those playing the race card are the small-minded individuals who engage in a broad stroke analysis of an entire group's behavior often from a negative perspective. The race card is often used to suggest racial implications that are not appropriate or accurate.

Many a black man can attest that their entry onto an elevator will cause some to double clutch their purses, as will walking down the same side of the street. However, those actions are not seen as playing the race card. And when the actions are pointed out by people of color they, the people of color, are identified as the ones playing the race card. Someone said I will stop playing the race card when people stop dealing it to me. Calling out racism in the face of racist behavior is not playing the race card. Calling out racism to defend against or hide from negative behavior just may be.

Consider a conversation where a merchant is in a meeting discussing the question: What is wrong with black people when they riot in their communities? (This is a legitimate question.) It appears that after every sporting championship, they riot and burn properties in their communities. "Why do black people riot all the time?" This type of conversation is an example of someone playing the race card to bring a broad stroke indictment against black people based on inaccurate information or inappropriate analysis.

The problem is that the speaker identified only black people regarding persons who riot after sporting championships. However, there is documented evidence of riots after sporting events and championships by other groups of people. Although they are often called overzealous celebrations, property damage is property damage. The foolish tendency to riot or loot because your team won a championship (or lost a big game) is not the exclusive prerogative of one group of people. This inappropriate behavior is a proclivity of a type of individual who perhaps feels voiceless, even in victory (or defeat). The turning over of vehicles, vandalizing of property, and setting fires is their way of expressing their excitement and frustration at life. Regardless of the reason for the action, it is not a race thing; it is a people thing.

Another common injection into conversations is the question: "Why can other groups come over here and make it and black people can't and have to go on welfare?" The truth of the matter is a sizable portion of the black community has made it despite the obstacles of racism. Not every black person has, but there are many who have become very successful in America even while experiencing racism in their lives. Those who make it often have stronger support networks or systems that help them or helped them at important decision points in their lives.

It may be as simple as having a father or mother who offered support when one was a child. Perhaps this occurred at a very important decision point in life, such as when someone stated to the child that she could be anything she wanted to be in life. Or perhaps she was allowed to attend a top scholastic institution giving her an excellent academic preparation. Many who don't become successful lack the support needed at critical junctures in their lives. However, at the same time and in spite of not always having support, there is a continued increase in the number of black people attending college, including black men, who are seeking to be part of the American mainstream and manifest the American dream and image of success.

Then, there are those who fit the stereotypes that support notions of inferiority, laziness, and the inability to work hard or take care of their responsibilities. Without question, there is a negative element present within the black community, just as there is a similar negative element in all communities. But this element is not the majority. Many persons who live at or below the poverty line are hardworking and seek to care for their families. Often persons who are struggling financially become targets for job down-sizing or the criminal justice system. Without a steady flow of legal income, fathers become separated from their families, thereby helping to feed the negative stereotypes of irresponsibility and abandonment.

Before playing the race card, the facts of the situation should be obtained, identified, assessed, discussed objectively, and compared to similarly situated scenarios or occurrences within other groups. One must objectively verify what happened, verify who was involved, ask how was this resolved in the past, and consider how was it resolved this time. Is there a pattern of different results based on who is involved? Before playing the race card, one must make sure all of the relevant facts are correct and available to determine the legitimacy of a judgment rendered based on race.

If there is a discernable pattern of different treatment, then there is a basis for making an assertion that racism is involved. Thus, in a corporate setting the punishment of one employee about punctuality while another is not punished may be due to racism but first look at all the factors. If one employee who brought in a big client is celebrated and another who brings in a big client is not, look at the factors. If one employee meets all of their objectives but fails to get a passing grade and another who missed on several objectives does get a passing grade or kudos for their efforts, look at the factors. If two employees are colleagues and the under-performing one gets the choice assignment or promotion, look at the factors. Let's identify the factors, look for patterns in behavior and name the truths as they are presented or discovered. And instead of lazily playing the race card, we must attempt to work to eliminate the problem, whether it is performance or racism that is present. The race card is not a trump card, and when played as if it is a trump card it is dangerous and divisive.

Chapter 3

BUILDING TRUST

*Honest communication is built on truth and integrity
and upon respect of the one for the other.*

– BENJAMIN E. MAYS

This statement by Dr. Benjamin E. Mays is critical to building trust. Without trust, an honest conversation about race will be a hard or impossible conversation to have. If groups are just people sharing space or functions without a sense of truth, integrity and respect for each other, they will have a difficult time discussing race or any other sensitive topic. As I stated in the introduction, when I was a young person entering the workforce, some of my co-workers made some rather outlandish remarks. Had I heard those remarks through one of my friends or acquaintances saying, "Do you know what some of the white people said at work…," I likely would have questioned their sanity. I would not have been as understanding. Depending on the subject, I would have summoned up my rage from countless negative encounters with white people and projected my rage onto the situation being reported to me and demanded resolution and a figurative pound of flesh from each person involved.

However, it was different when I experienced the "outlandish remarks" at work and in person. The reason persons in our group could say what we said to each other and not have flared tempers was because we had established a level of trust and respect with one another as we made this exploration into adulthood. We trusted one another to say what we said about our then-current worldviews based on deep northern-styled segregation. The racism that we experienced in Chicago was real. Intuitively, we knew that the only way to move forward was to say what was on our minds or in our hearts. We learned to trust that it would be okay to say it, and place it on the table for discussion.

We didn't work with established anti-racism workgroup guidelines. We didn't have a contract that we signed stating this is a safe environment. We didn't have a set procedure on how we would share our understandings or worldviews. We just did it. We said things honestly; there was no name calling; we were not antagonistic; we were just open and honest.

Also, the language of the neighborhoods was left in the neighborhood. We were young; we were becoming friends, and we trusted each other. That trust allowed us to get our work collectively completed. Perhaps we were just naïve, but it worked; we could say almost anything to one another because of the trust level. And we learned from one another that certain words or expressions caused pain. Because of the value of our relationships, we learned that some of our childhood views and expressions were no longer useful. So some of the language of the neighborhood was left in our neighborhoods. We didn't always agree on every point of view expressed, but we were always free to be vulnerable. We were able to let our guards down so we could talk and have honest conversations that reduced our bigotry, and we became friends.

Trust is essential to the discussion of race. Without trust, a sustainable conversation is impossible. Trust is required to accept another's clarity about their blind spots, or one's delusions about self or one's self-identifying group. It is difficult for a white counterpart's biting comments about a person of color to be heard by a person of color and accepted unless trust between the two has been established. And in today's world of social media, the comments made to a friend read and by those without established trust becomes fodder to feed the incendiary machine of racial bias and animus.

Thus, when a person introduces a topic for discussion on social media and the vitriolic comments flow, it is because the trust is not there between the responders and the person who made the comment. The unfiltered responses made in the social media environment are often troubling and vindictive and are not useful for moving the needle towards racial harmony.

Consider this scenario: Ann, the white supervisor, wants to tell Carl the black employee that his performance is sub-par. If Carl does not trust her, she will need documentation to support the claim. Otherwise, her remarks may be interpreted as racist, especially if Jim a white employee is praised and his work level is perceived to be on par with Carl's.

Perception is subjective based on the observer's ability to understand what they observe. Those with white racial bias will see flaws in Carl while missing those same flaws with Jim. Right now, some readers are in disagreement with this statement because they have not developed trust with me. But that is the nature of bias, to see stimuli in any given situation in a manner that supports our view of the truth and our claims of perception. Here's a case in point. Your favorite sports team makes a great play, but the official calls a penalty against your team. When you saw that play, you saw the activity in favor of your team. Even the official offering indisputable proof may not matter to your perception.

Being accused of interfering with a catch in the 2003 Major League Baseball playoffs for the Chicago Cubs, Steve Bartman was a hated man in Chicago. Clearly the replay shows that he was standing near the foul line in the left-field seats. As the ball came towards Steve, several other people made attempts at getting the baseball. In other words, several people made attempts at interfering with the play. But the ball was coming directly towards Steve, and because there was contact with him and the ball, he is blamed for the

Cubs losing the game and subsequently the playoffs and, once again, not going to the World Series. I bet many a Cub fan will refuse to believe otherwise, and some may even refuse to buy this book because of this reference to bias. It was not his goal to intentionally interfere with the play and cause the Cubs to lose that game. But for thousands of Cub fans, they will not see it any other way.

The point is this: Unexamined perception is biased – which some may call implicit bias. When one is unaware that one is biased, it often results in challenging the possibility of honest conversation and trust. So when Ann tells Carl his work is sloppy, Carl wants to know about Jim's work. And instead of understanding that he needs improvement he may lash out and claim that he is being treated unfairly because of his race (Yes, he is playing the race card!).

However, if Carl's perception of Ann is positive and he has trust for Ann, Carl will respect Ann's opinion and will respond with a thanks for the heads up. Carl will work harder so that his work will meet the company's standards and Ann's approval regardless of Jim's performance. Now as the boss Ann doesn't need trust; she can just lay out her documentation to support the evaluation and set improvement goals for Carl to meet. But with trust Ann could make the comments and know that a word to the wise is sufficient.

Trust does not mean holding hands and singing songs together; it just means that one is understood to be fair and unbiased in their dealings with counterparts. Ann can't be the only one in the relationship thinking that she is fair. Being fair or trustworthy is not a reputation that one can give oneself; one has to earn it. And one of the quickest ways to *not* have that reputation earned is to claim it for oneself.

Trust is not always an easy thing to establish. We live in a world of connected isolation; some workgroups only come together via video chat or online documents. The face to face chat is more and more a text message, a post, a webcast, a tweet, or an email. Trust helps one to build a tolerance for other people; thus, trust, integrity, and tolerance are the main ingredients in the recipe for honest conversation. True conversations are those where persons are willing to listen to each other as persons. Trust involves real listening, not the just waiting for the other person to stop speaking so one can say what one wants to say. Honest and true conversation leads to effective communication; one has moved from hearing to active listening because one cares. And once people care, they have the basis for displaying integrity. As they build up their sense of integrity, they can tear down the walls of bias that separate people. They can then begin to impact the heart disease of bigotry. Thus, what gets in the way of trust is a lack of integrity and respect for the other person, and holding on to learned biases and personal prejudices that become dubious universal truths about others.

To build the level of trust needed to have deep conversations about race, one's communication must be honest and free of bias, as often represented by microaggressions or statements that indicate an unperceived but nevertheless present bias. If Carl hears, Ann saying, let's "circle the wagons," or refer to a defeat as a "massacre" when it is her favorite team losing and a "victory" when they win; or if Carl hears Ann's remarks about the ubiquitous "black hole," and one is not talking about gravity or space, but simply about not finding something on her desk, Ann may not be as bias-free as she thinks she is.

Consider Bob the manager going on and on about a blacklist and black ball or black hole, and because he is the boss, no one challenges him about his choice of words that convey negativity. If Teri makes a comment, she may be told that she is too sensitive. What if Teri said, "Okay, I just didn't want to whitewash the issue," and then Bob, the manager, gets mad at the negative use of the word "white?" One of the best ways to build trust is to have honest communication and accept feedback regarding the areas that we can't see or sometimes just take for granted.

Once trust is established, honest communication will grow as long as integrity is maintained. One of the impediments to building trust and honest communication is the risk of being vulnerable to others. Thus, building trust can and is often a risky behavior, a behavior that doesn't always come easy in a workplace environment where perception itself is a commodity for advancement or demotion. For the brave the reward of risk is to be the leader and trusted counsel for your group.

Now in the workplace, to facilitate trust often there has to be buy-in from the executive levels. If the C-Level executives of the business will exhibit the required behavior, then those down the line will feel less vulnerable and will be more open to taking the risk required for change. Thus, executive level buy-in is crucial for a critical mass of employees to move in the desired direction towards honest conversation. Once trust is established, the communication needed to improve employee performance without the fear of bias and bigotry is possible. Once trust is established, when one has to correct an employee or counterpart it will be a much easier task. And once the critical mass of trust is commonplace, bigotry begins to fall and the organization can begin to dismantle racist policies both private and corporate. We can't legislate trust, but with trust the successful removal of hate and bigotry from existing policies and behaviors can be achieved. With trust, we can help to eradicate racism and the notion and effects of white supremacy from our world faster than legislation and protracted litigation.

Chapter 4

ORIGINS OF RACISM

Racism and injustice and violence sweep our world,
bringing a tragic harvest of heartache and death.

— *Billy Graham*

R acism is born of bigotry and is the economic engine of white supremacy.
Without racism, white supremacy would lose its power. It was the need
to make white supremacy profitable that spawned the notions of race and racism. And once it became profitable racism has sustained white supremacy, has
kept it profitable, and has made it too big to fail easily.

Laurel Schneider writes:

Europeans vied for control of the world in pursuit of greater economic
gain and dominance over trade. The emergence of colonial capitalism
with its emphasis on private property fueled the search for a rationale
for acquiring cheaper and cheaper labor, with outright ownership of
labor being the ideal. Scientific theories of race served both acquisitive

goals for the most part substantiating convictions that preceded scientific inquiry.[4]

White Supremacy is the false notion that whiteness is inherently better than blackness or any other color or hue found in the human race. Currently, the world, as Schneider points out, is under a colonialist white rule that provides power, privilege, and profit for being white. But that profit does not mean there is an inherent or natural superiority of white people over other people, in spite of the voices of white supremacy that argue otherwise. White supremacy is a system supported by established systemic and institutionalized practices of propaganda, a bigoted pedagogy, and violence. White supremacy has an entrenched stronghold on societal resources and the American mindset.

The foundational origins for racism and white supremacy are bigotry and power for profit. At the core of white supremacy are the lies that there is more than one human race and that one race is superior to all others. Force and violence support the propaganda, and for those who adhere to the politics of racism they are rewarded with protection and financial gain or prosperity. In other words, white supremacy is at its core a wealth supremacy system protected by racism.

The beginning of white supremacy starts with the bigotry that one ethnic group is superior to another ethnic group based solely on the genetic characteristic of skin color. White skin does not make one superior to another. The system of white supremacy provides advantages to white people but not inherent superiority. And that system is maintained through miseducation, privilege, and power.

---

4 Laurel Schneider, "White People On What We Need To Do; Essay What Race Is Your Sex," in *Disrupting White Supremacy from Within, editors,* Jennifer Harvey, Karin A. Case, and Robin Hawley Gorsline, Cleveland, OH: Pilgrim Press, 2004, 152

Dr. Jacqueline Battalora writes from a legal perspective regarding the birth of white supremacy:

> The shift from "English and other freeborn women" to "English and other *white* women and men" as the class requiring protection is significant. The Maryland law of 1681 reflects the first time in legal history, in the land that would eventually become the U.S., that "white" was used in law to reflect a human classification. This Maryland law represents the invention of "white" people in law.[5]

One of the major ingredients in the formation of white supremacy was establishing a pedagogy or system of beliefs that concluded white people were superior to other people. One of the key factors in this notion was the development of race theory. The claim is that there are several different races, each with innate characteristics, levels of intelligence, skin tone that makes each one different and better than another. Thus, a specific pseudo-scientific theory was developed to support the notion that the white race was superior to other races.[6]

This belief of superiority established through means of education and military actions devalued the humanity of the so-called "lower race(s)." Once devalued as people, their rights were also negated to the point that they no longer have any rights that the superior group has to respect. As a result, what belongs to the devalued group is now available for the taking by the valued group.

Laurel Schneider further makes the case that the dominant white race sees itself as masculine while viewing all other colonized races as feminine, and thus diminished in relation to the white race that by virtue of their collective masculinity has the right to rule over non-white feminine races.[7]

---

5 Jacqueline Battalora, *Birth of a White Nation*, Houston, TX: Strategic Book Publishing and Rights Co., 2013, 25.

6 Schneider, 155.

7 Ibid., 156.

Consider that Indians or sovereign tribes lived in this area called the Turtle Islands, but that was later changed to America. They inhabited this land before the Europeans came and settled. When European settlers or immigrants came and became entrenched, the new inhabitants felt empowered to take from these native people their ancestral lands. Without a qualm, the new immigrants engaged in ruthless behaviors to force the native populations off their homelands. Under the pretext of advancement and progress, the United States Government removed the existing native dwellers from their homelands, reinforcing the notion of masculine dominance. Once this sense of superiority was established, those who were considered superior fought to protect their status. Therefore, alleged superior status, miseducation, and violence are key elements in sustaining notions of white supremacy and the sense that 'might makes right.'

By the method of devaluing the other or people of color, persons who were indigenous to Africa were seized to attend to the development of the nascent American colonies. Again, because of the theory of white supremacy, there was no need to value the rights of others, so people of color were available to be used as needed by the white race. As the colonies were becoming the Americas, cheap labor was required to make the economies of the colonies succeed. The initial round of cheap labor was other white people, often of the "lower" white races (ethnic groups) or classes. These persons exchanged their labor for a defined period of time, passage, and a promise of a better life. However, the hardships of the rigorous labor produced resentment. Many of the white indentured servants prematurely escaped to lands towards the western frontiers, leaving the places where they were indentured to blend into their new settings. By prematurely escaping from their indentured servitude, and thereby reducing the time of servitude, the practice of using white indentured servants became unprofitable to the land and business owners. Likewise, forcing native people into the same labor efforts also proved to be unprofitable. The natives would simply escape back into familiar surroundings, and the attempts to recapture them were often unfruitful. Thus, a more permanent solution was sought.

Dr. Claud Anderson writes of the racial perspectives that developed as an element of white supremacy:

> Black enslavement was the first instance in history that had a world-wide collaborative, race-oriented support for slave trading. Prior to the 15th century, slavery was more of a one-to-one phenomenon: warrior to warrior, nation to nation. Never had there been a situation where all white nations of Europe were collectively against blacks on the African continent.[8]

In 1619, the first group of indentured servants from Africa came to America and the problems of sustained cheap labor was presented with a solution. Here was a group of people who were forced to endure the hard work, because they could not simply run off and not be detected. Their skin color was a mark that identified them and made it almost impossible to escape and, thus, perfect for permanent enslavement.[9]

Prior to Bacon's Rebellion in 1676 indentured workers, regardless of color, were treated in a similar negative manner and posed a "threat of a united labor force." The ruling class responded by creating groups allowing one group to have "authority to rule over and oppress the other."[10]

A few decades after the introduction of the first African indentured servants in 1619, it became the law of the land that African persons brought to the Americas as a source of labor would have a status of a permanent servant or slave. The problem of finding a permanent cheap labor source was solved. Further the laws regarding marriage changed and made it illegal for blacks and whites to marry. The legal way to determine lineage changed from fathers to mothers; these changes in the law created a situation where by law the children of an enslaved mother were born into slavery. This change opened the

---

8   Claud Anderson, *Black Labor, White Wealth*, Edgewood, MD: Duncan & Duncan, Inc., 1994, 69.

9   Battalora, 23.

10   Battalora, 19.

door for white men to increase their number of slaves by raping the enslaved mothers. These acts of rape served to increase profit margins and reinforced the decision to make permanent servitude or enslavement as property the status for black people.[11]

Further, reducing the enslaved person to the status of property absolved whites from any feelings of guilt for their mistreatment of other human beings. White supremacy developed racism to be its economic engine, and it has achieved its goal by producing goods and services at a maximized profit. Since African people were considered sub-human by the emerging culture of white supremacy their enslavement was not an ethical problem.

To reinforce the notion of black inferiority, and to draw attention away from the political process that created this classification both pseudo-scientific and pseudo-biblical warrants were created. These pseudo-warrants served the white supremacy culture by stating that enslavement for blacks was part of the natural order of things.

Howard Zinn counters the warrant of a natural order of things and supports the perspective that white was a created status and that enslavement entrapped free Africans for profit:

> We see a complex web of historical threads to ensnare blacks for slavery in America: the desperation of starving settlers, the special helplessness of the displaced African, the powerful incentive for profit for slave trader and planter, the temptation of superior status for poor whites, the elaborate controls against escape and rebellion, the legal and social punishment of black and white collaboration.

---

11 Ibid., 10.

The point is that the elements of this web are historical, not "natural."[12]

The web that Zinn describes points to an America not founded by white people for white people, but of an America founded by wealthy white people for other wealthy white people. The classification of white was opened to include poor white people to ensure the success of the colonial economy. This understanding reinforces the earlier point that white supremacy is a wealth supremacy system. Chattel slavery is no longer part of our landscape, yet the bigotry and racism that allowed its birth remains.

---

12 Howard Zinn, *A People's History of the United States*, New York, NY: HarperPerennial, 2003, 38.

Chapter 5

THE ALLEGED COLORBLINDNESS
OF A POST-RACIAL AMERICA

The more you know your history, the more liberated you are.

— Maya Angelou

We live in this era of a so-called post-racial America, and we see black people at every level of achievement in our society, including serving as The President of the United States of America. Even as black and other people of color have risen in levels of achievement in our society, the process of a negative pedagogy remains.

What we have seen since the election of President Obama is a rise of public hate rhetoric and a revising of American history. There is a new propaganda machine that suggests that slavery was a good thing for black people and that anything goes when it comes to attacking black people, including The President, in the public media. These attacks help to reinforce the mindset that whites are innately superior to blacks and other people of color.

Today in the "post-racist America" some people acknowledge that racism existed, but say that they are not racist. Further, many people say that racism today is not nearly as bad as it was in the 60s or previously. I believe that things are not as bad outwardly as they were at the dawn of the Civil Rights era for black people. Black people have made significant strides in claiming a piece of the American pie of success. I imagine that some who may be reading this have a supervisor who is of color. But these strides and success do not negate that work has to continue to get to a point where the effects of white supremacy and racism are further minimized and eradicated in our society. Consider a pot of half cooked rice; it has moved along but it is still not finished or suitable for eating; there is still cooking or work to be done.

One of the biggest problems in eradicating racism is the current sense of good race relations. The book *Good to Great* suggests "good is the enemy of great." When organizations get to good – because they have achieved profit margins, market penetration, and employee bonuses – they are seen as having achieved the pinnacle of success. In truth, they have done the work, but they have not gotten to the finish line; there is still a goal of the better left to achieve.[13] Having a multi-racial group of drinking buddies is not equality, having an integrated sorority or fraternity, hiring more people of color, or even removing a symbol of hate are all good starts but are not the great finish that we seek. Good is better than where we were, but it is not as great as it can be.

In a recent on-line article, Mychal Denzel Smith says, "Millennials are fluent in colorblindness and diversity while remaining illiterate in the language of anti-racism." Being anti-racism-illiterate paves the way for their belief that "racism is a relic of the past." Smith believes that it is partially the fault of Baby Boomers and Gen-Xers who taught that racism is a matter of personal bigotry and not institutional power.[14] While I can see his point about Millennials, I will have to question Smith on the point of Baby Boomers'

13 Jim Collins, *Good to Great*, New York, NY: Harper Collins Publishers 2001, 16.
14 Mychal Denzel Smith, "White Millennials Are Products of a Failed Lesson in Colorblindness" *Race Today*, March 26, 2015, PBS.org.

misunderstanding. Many Baby Boomers who were the recipients of better education and better employment opportunities than their parents did try to distance themselves from the struggle against racism. Many a person – after finding themselves living the "American Dream" – bought into the pull yourself up by the bootstrap myth. But their success, regardless of their talent, was never a solo enterprise; it was in part purchased by the blood of those who died walking dusty roads to fight for equality. Regarding the cause and sustainability of racism, not all Baby-Boomers are misled, especially those involved in the Civil Rights demonstrations in the 60s, who continued to demonstrate in the 70s and 80s. There are many Baby Boomers who fully understand the power dynamic and have remained involved with eradicating racism in one form or another.

The perceptions amongst those who believe that racism is over, or that reverse racism is real, arise from the pedagogy of denial. The perceptions are a symptom of the lingering effects of racism and feed the sense that racism is dead, enabling some people to feel good about the current ideology of racial progress. But events occur that shake the perceptions, and the vivid reality of racism returns to the forefront. Yes, it is better for most people of color, and we have made racial progress. But we can't be so comfortable that we stop trying to make things systemically and institutionally better, because there is still much work to be done. Until one realizes that good is representative of complacency or a narcotic vision of inclusion, there will remain an illusion of free and willful participation in our society.

The key to the belief in a new non-racist society is the 'It's not my fault mantra,' a belief that there are no tangible lingering effects of racism in our world for which anyone is responsible. There is a disbelief by the new "non-racist" persons that systems are still in place to trap people of color into poverty and second-class citizenry. The so-called new non-racists assert that because slavery happened more than a century ago it is not their responsibility to address it and that black people should get over the period of chattel slavery. Thus, the colorblindness expressed is also blindness to the intentionality of racialized policies that persist in our society. Racism is an insidious infection that seeks to limit or truncate the desires and possibilities of many persons of color. Racism serves to redirect them toward futures that are aimless and hopeless, making them perfect candidates for a permanent underclass that will make up future prison populations or cheap labor. The influence of violence themed anti-police music of the 80s and early 90s, the disproportionate number of blacks arrested and sentenced for violations of drug laws, and the proliferation of prison construction produced a perfect storm or triangulation directed towards the black community. And once a person becomes a convicted felon, reentry to mainstream society is severely hampered.

But, let us look at the concept of that 'it's in the past; just let it go.' The legacy of slavery could have been exhausted or resolved if the period of Reconstruction started in the 1860s had run its course. But because Reconstruction ended in 1877, the resolution was truncated. The period of Reconstruction lost its power and was replaced by another harmful system – Jim Crow – designed to produce cheap black labor. According to Michelle Alexander, and others, Jim Crow is still very much a part of the fabric of our society.[15] Racism is still problematic, and the lingering effects of slavery that gave rise to its existence still harm people of color.

I remember speaking with people who had experienced a bad sunburn and who stated that it was painful. I have heard people talking about feeling like a lobster. They furthered expressed that sometimes it took days after they were exposed to a sunburn before the pain subsided. They were experiencing the lingering effects of the sunburn. The lingering effects of the sunburn, even days after the event, caused areas of their bodies to be too painful to be touched. What would have happened if they would have gone back out into the sunlight and exposed themselves to another sunburn before the existing sunburn had a chance to heal?

---

15   Michelle Alexander, *The New Jim Crow: Mass Incarceration in the Age of Colorblindness*, New York, NY: The New Press, 2010, 2012.

We didn't always know, but now there has been enough education to warn the general public that prolonged exposure to the sun, because of harmful UV rays, can produce skin cancer. Skin cancer from prolonged exposure to the harmful rays of the sun could be considered a result or lingering effect of the sunburn that occurred in the past. Once detected cancer treatment would be required to fight this result. How would one treat cancer? Would one follow the doctor's recommendations? Would one follow them to the letter, or would one decide only to follow some of them? What if the doctor's recommendations provided only 3/5ths of the treatments needed? What if one's insurance company denied the treatments? What if access to the treatment center was blocked and one had to delay or cancel the treatments?

What if this happened to you? How would you feel about the lingering effects of something that happened in the past? What if, after having begun treatments, the staff at the facility had changed and when you got there you found out that the people in charge of administering your treatments were incompetent and had given you the wrong medication for your condition? What if they just didn't care about you and made you wait all day only to send you home without your treatment and told you to come back next week? What if they just ran out of your medications and said we don't know when another shipment will arrive? What if you were treated inhumanely during your so-called healing process? Could the sunburn from a week, a month, two months, or a year ago have any lingering effects or consequences? The answer to these questions is yes. Events of the past can have lingering effects, and prolonged exposure to the initial cause or stimuli produces a greater period of lingering and potential harm.

For those who are thinking, "If I chose to go back into the sun then that is my fault," consider this. What if you did not have the agency to make a choice and act accordingly? What if you were forced to go out into the sun unprotected every day for a month? What then? What if there was a deliberate plan to cause you to get sunburned because there was an industry, a sunburn industry that existed for the sole purpose of giving people sunburn?

And another that existed for treating it? What if the economy of a nation was based on giving some people sunburns and all those involved in giving those sunburns were paid or rewarded because of your sunburn?

The point is, we live in a world where slavery is acknowledged but the legacy, the lingering effects are not. The legacy of slavery has produced ongoing effects that have created a tiered society where race is still a factor. The large number of persons trapped in poverty is not a simple matter of the less industrious being poor while the achievers and more industrious persons are rich or middle class. That could be in a true colorblind society. And that is the goal, but in reality there are still systems and institutionalized restraints in place that help to maintain racism based on skin color in our so-called colorblind society.

In today's world, there is a glaring desire to not take ownership of the legacy of slavery, while many persons are enjoying the benefits of it. Today people of color do have more options for advancement and success than a generation or two ago. But to deny that racism is alive or that racism is irrelevant is a delusion, a denial. Even the success of people of color does not negate the systemic application of bias and bigotry in our nation and world and that there are those who still benefit from it. Notwithstanding the reality that persons with access to successful treatments and medications may be treated for their sunburn and overcome it, the fact remains that just because someone recovered from an illness does not mean the disease has been eradicated if others are still getting sick. The achievement of limited healing does not mean the disease no longer exists. The reality that there is a black elected President of the United States of America or other blacks who have successful careers does not imply that racism in America is over.

Chapter 6

THE USE OF LANGUAGE TO CONTINUE WHITE SUPREMACY

*The color of the skin is in no way connected with
strength of the mind or intellectual powers.*

– Benjamin Banneker

Part of the conversation of colorblindness includes the concept "the new Black." One of the expressions that I heard from someone who identified themselves as being a *"new Black"* was a restating of the "people need to pull themselves up by their bootstraps" mantra, that there are too many opportunities in today's society for some to not do well as they did not take advantage, that failure to be successful is an individual's fault and not a systemic issue. Those who identify themselves as representing the new Black believe, as do others who express that they are colorblind, that anyone who does not succeed in this society has not tried or is just lazy. In other words shame on those who fail, they made that choice.

One of the tools of racism in a colorblind society is to stigmatize methods that help to reduce racism. Thus, one of the strongest and most insidious tools in the arsenal of white supremacy is the powerful use of stigmas. Stigmas are used to create a culture of refusal to employ tools and language that can help dismantle racism and the negative effects of white supremacy. These stigmas that are employed to produce shaming have the effect of making the process to dismantle racism and white supremacy too hot to touch. It is like leaving a metal hammer out in the sun all day on a hot day, with the result that when one goes to pick it up with their bare hands, they will get burned. To touch it, to pick it up requires gloves, but, in this case, the use of gloves is also stigmatized or covered in a dung of shame and is also off limits.

Two terms cloaked in stigmatizations are "affirmative action" and "victim." Stigmatized terms lose their effective power to hammer away at the structures of racism and white supremacy, because once they are stigmatized, those who use them, those who invoke them, are confronted with the intention of stigmatization: to bring cultural shame to anyone who employs them. Whenever there is a collective effort to stigmatize a tool, an understanding, a process, or a term, we know there must be a value to it. I remember in the 50s a little store in my neighborhood where the grocer didn't want to return change to the shoppers especially the children often saying it is only a penny. "It is only" was designed to bring shame to the shopper who wanted that penny and to convey that they were so poor they had to argue over a penny. I was told, by my parents, to get all of the change. So I insisted on that penny, or two, and I began to realize that if those pennies were important to him, then they should have been important to me as well. It was important. If he could shame people out of their change, it was extra unearned profit for the grocer and an added burden or tax upon the people in the neighborhood.

The term "Affirmative Action" was coined by President John F. Kennedy in Executive Order 10925. The term was designed to be an intentional effort at including talented and qualified under-represented persons into the job pool and workforce. In less than 20 years, it was made into a term of shame. To be viewed as an affirmative action hire was turned into a negative. It became a mark of shame because being an affirmative action hire was stigmatized to convey that one was not quite good enough to make it on their own.

Now there are some persons who were beneficiaries of Affirmative Action programs of the 60s and 70s who by the 80s believed in the obsolescence of Affirmative Action programs. They yielded to the shaming power of the pedagogy of a "colorblind" culture. The term Affirmative Action carries with it a stigma of not being good enough to compete at the same level. There are persons of color as well as others who have benefitted from Affirmative Action programs, but some now desire to distance themselves from the idea because the implied stigma devalues the accomplishments of those who benefitted from such programs. Today we use terms like diversity and multicultural – the latter of which often really means multi-racial but mono-cultural – in place of Affirmative Action because of the stigma attached to being an Affirmative Action recipient or "baby."

Affirmative Action programs were meant to find qualified persons who came from environments that have or had been overlooked, ignored, and or underserved. The programs were designed to give deserving people an equal opportunity to compete in places of prior denial.

The education programs offered in the 60s have produced some of America's brightest scholars. The programs that enabled business professionals from underserved and under-represented communities to have access to lucrative government contracts and careers in corporate America also produced a bumper crop of excellent performers who became excellent role models for those coming behind them. As for those in the military, some of our top commanders were the beneficiaries of those early efforts that allowed them access and the opportunity to compete. And once they were eligible to compete they excelled and dispelled the popular and racist notions of inherent inferiority.

By the late 70s and early 80s, many Blacks had benefitted from Affirmative Action. Those who had benefitted began to feel as if their achievements were being given the "side-eye," that their achievements were noted with an asterisk. The problem may have been that the programs were too successful and that without bringing some measure of shame and divisiveness there may have been an overrun of unintended success. And those who were traditionally given these opportunities (some without merit) may suddenly have experienced the pain of being left behind because of their lack of qualifications.

Thus, there was an attack on the programs in the 1970s. Lawsuits and a pedagogy of shame were developed. The programs were being called quota programs to imply that undeserving persons of color were getting positions that belonged to, without any evidence except skin color, more qualified whites. President Kennedy introduced Affirmative Action but it was through The Civil Rights Act of 1964 that created the Equal Employment Opportunity Commission under President Lyndon Johnson that real and tangible efforts were being established to provide opportunity to historically underserved communities of color. Arthur Fletcher, called the Father of Affirmative Action, developed the Philadelphia Plan in 1970 while working in President Nixon's administration. This plan provided structure to affirmative action programs by introducing regulations and vendor practices for those bidding for Government contracts.

By 1978 Affirmative Action policies in higher education were under attack. These attacks successfully imposed a stigma on the term "Affirmative Action" and served to neutralize a sense of pride about one's talent and performance being recognized. Being a recipient of an Affirmative Action program benefit was now considered negative, and persons were supposed to forego such help and "pull themselves up by their bootstraps."

To pull oneself up by one's bootstraps is part of the American myth of the rugged individual. This sentiment that America based its success on the fortitude of rugged individuals who braved the frontiers of resistance and forged out of the granite landscapes structures based on an individual's personal grit is overstated. There were persons of vision and intestinal fortitude that took the raw materials of this great land and made America the great bastion of independence and personal achievement that we have before us. But they all had systemic help. We have images of log cabins and men and women with their flintlocks, coonskin caps and covered wagons all fueled by grit that ushered in the greatness that has become the legacy and heritage that is America. But the ruggedness of individuals united for a common purpose that overcame all obstacles without the help of big government or special programs is a myth.

The truth of these efforts is that America employed the use of race-based government policies for the benefit of white people. Those race-based programs do not and have never carried with them a negative connotation or stigma. In fact, some people speak with great pride of the race-based programs that established, that helped to create and maintain their family's wealth. Let us consider the following list of a few examples in regard to the myth of the rugged individual and the use of big government race-based programs or group practices that helped white people in America:

* *Indian Treaties and the Removal Act of 1830.* This act made it possible for Indians to be forcibly removed by the U.S. government from their lands east of the Mississippi River and given to white settlers in exchange for land west of the Mississippi River.
* *The Homestead Act of 1862.* This act made it possible for the U. S. government to take land west of the Mississippi River from Indians and give it to white settlers in exchange for new smaller homelands now called reservations.
* *The Supreme Court decision Dred Scott v. Sandford.* This decision took away the expectation of black people to be considered citizens of the United States. Justice Taney, in his opinion for the highest court in the land, wrote that blacks were "beings of an inferior order so far inferior, which they had no rights that the white man was bound to respect."
* *Hayes-Tilden Compromise.* This Congressional compromise called for the immediate removal of federal troops from the South that served as a protection for the newly freed black persons. That essentially ended the period of Reconstruction, in 1877, where black people were pulling themselves up by their bootstraps in business and politics.
* *Race Riots and Lynching. Race Riots* started by white people served as an effective means to subdue the emergence of black people from a

permanent underclass. Some race riots of note during the early 20th century are the Atlanta Race Riots of 1906 and the Chicago Race Riot of 1919 which were two of more than two dozens that year. Additional major riots include the Tulsa Race Riot of 1921 that destroyed what was called Black Wall Street, an area of thriving commerce in the black community. *Lynching* served to promote white supremacy and control black achievement and was a permanent and ubiquitous threat. It served as a deterrent to black self-determination and remained as the ever-present spark to a powder-keg of white reprisal against the black achievement. The ever-present rumor that a black man had inappropriately addressed a white woman often ignited lynchings and white riots. This "inappropriate" address could have been an alleged rape, or an unwanted touch, a whistle or even a look that may have never taken place. Thousands of black men and women were lynched during the 19th and 20th centuries. It is this writer's strong belief that the actual number of black people lynched in the United States will never be known. One French writer commented that lynchings were so numerous that when blacks saw poplar trees they had to imagine a black person hanging from their limbs. Billie Holiday addressed this phenomenon in the song "Strange Fruit."

Picture a beautiful full moonlit sky on a mid-spring night. The moon is so full you could see the craters as it appears to sit on top of the ridge. Suddenly there is a sound of horses and men laughing on top of the ridge just below the moon. The men are congratulating themselves before they depart and go their separate ways down the hill; one is coming closer, his noble steed at full gallop. As he draws closer, his face shielded against the night air by a hooded mask, he shouts, and the door opens. The rider disembarks and a woman greets him with a loving and passionate embrace; the children set the table with food to feed their father. And over the ridge following slowly behind the night rider are the screams of a wife, mother, and child, now fatherless, who have discovered the strange fruit in their yard.

Often lynchings were public events as evidenced by scores of postcards and photos from the early 1900s. The term "picnic" is said to be a conflation of "pick a nigger" which indicated there would be a public lynching. The term served as an invitation for people to bring food to enjoy the event; lynchings were a family affair.

* *Redlining.* Another tangible example of systemic and institutionalized racism (or government support that privileged the mythical "rugged individual,") was redlining, the practice of designating some areas to be serviced fairly by a banking institution while restricting those services to other groups and areas based on race. If persons of a group are directed to live in a geographical area and that area is designated to not receive funding or institutional support redlining has occurred. The term redlining comes from practices of the housing and insurance industries that drew red lines around some communities and denied resources to those communities. Redlining would target the black community especially, and banks could withhold mortgages or business loans from members of redlined areas, or if they allowed the loans they would be at a higher rate than for communities that were not targeted. Redlining had a dramatic impact on individuals within that community. The denial of funds also meant denied monies for higher education, a business loan, or home improvement. Redlining ensured that equality would have to wait.

These are but a few examples of the ways the United States government, businesses and other groups engaged in, supported, or turned a blind eye to events or policies that were race-based and benefited white Americans to the detriment of persons of color, while culturally claiming the myth of the rugged individual.

Another term that is used to create a stigma is the term victim. When black people lay out a detailed and honest representation of the historical events that were designed to produce a permanent black underclass, white people will often say something to the effect "You poor victim." The word victim is thus meant to be a stigma and precludes the continued address of the horrors initiated against black people and other people of color in the Americas. The pursuit to stigmatize this term when applied to the brutal mistreatment of black people and others helps to form a condition of a deniability of the advantages that white people have inherited based on their skin color. If the term victim is stigmatized, it will help to foster a polarization between well-meaning whites and persons of color, creating an end run around any culpability in the mistreatment of persons of color while allowing the enjoyment of white skin privileges.

The term victim – often coupled with assertions such as "When my grandfather arrived here he was penniless, and yet he worked to build a successful business" – is used to imply black people are in the predicament that they are in because of their lack of initiative and hard work, that racism had and has nothing to do with the problems that black people face. Another chant used to deflect the lingering impact of racism is to say, "Look at all of the black people who are successful. If racism still existed why did Oprah have such a successful career? Why is Tyler Perry a household name? Why was a black president able to be elected?" These events have nothing to do with the planned, systematic, and institutionalized efforts to oppress people of color or racism. Again, if a person contracts a deadly disease and can overcome the disease that does not mean the disease no longer exists.

There is a book called *The New Black* which is a collection of 11 essays written by leading black educators, attorneys, and an economist. Perhaps the most recognizable name would belong to Lani Guinier, the first woman of color appointed to a tenured professorship at Harvard Law School and who was a nominee for Assistant Attorney General for Civil Rights in 1993 by then President Clinton. The book is designed to look at "what has changed and what has not with race in America." Dr. Orlando Patterson, a cultural sociologist and professor at Harvard, writes in the preface "One must be skeptical about measuring the progress toward racial equality by the emergence of successful blacks. As John Hope Franklin noted, the role of successful blacks in American society may be merely to ensure 'that there is sufficient sway in

America's still racist structure to provide the "give" necessary to protect that structure against the winds.'"[16]

Regardless of the success of persons of color we have been the victims of horrible crimes against humanity. We cannot allow the term victim to be stigmatized. We must claim and embrace it regardless of our current status.

In other words, if there are no victims of past behavior it becomes plausible to expect a cultural attitude of no victim no crime. Thus, a continued pseudo-innocence and deniability of the legacy of injustice remains. We must not allow ourselves to throw away the terms affirmative action or victim. Any person who claims an inheritance of wealth from a family member is not ashamed to be called an heir, nor is there shame or stigmatization when the term legacy is applied to a person who attends their parent's alma mater with guaranteed admission.

We cannot allow white people the luxury of being naïve about their privilege and other benefits derived from racism. We must remain vigilant to the claims of innocence and redirect them to awareness of their inherited benefit of *white privilege*, a term coined by Dr. Peggy McIntosh.[17] Thus, we need to understand that as a collective, black people here in the Americas were victims of a system that enslaved them for the group and personal gain of white people. Even as victims we have fought against the system of injustice to survive and to thrive. Yes, we are victims of hate, bigotry, and racism but we have not remained helpless or hopeless. We embraced and exercised power as a collective and as individuals to achieve goals and the status of success in a bigotry filled and oppressive environment. Affirmative Action programs created cracks in the walls of segregation, racism, and victimization. And those who were able to take full advantage of those programs, like Title IX in sports, did so because of their desire to achieve and because they had the ability to

---

16 Orlando Patterson, "Preface," *The New Black,* editors Kenneth W. Mack and Guy-Uriel E. Charles, New York, NY: The New Press, 2013, xi.

17 Peggy McIntosh. "White Privilege and Male Privilege: A Personal Account of Coming to See Correspondence Through Women's Studies." Wellesley, MA: Wellesley College, 1988.

compete to obtain success. Affirmation action is not an entitlement program; rather, it is an effort to extend fairness to unfairly treated and underserved people mostly because of the color of their skin.

Racism in America was and is fueled by bigotry and entrenched by race-based Government programs. This combination firmly established white supremacy as the dominant thought pattern in our society. And there is evidence that these systems of domination have continued, perhaps under different names and strategies, but the need to maintain a system of cheap black (and people of color) labor has been maintained and continues. For the colorblind individuals who ask has there been progress in racial relations in America, the answer is a resounding yes. But has it been enough to overturn the nearly 400 years of servitude, slavery, Jim Crow, Segregation, and white supremacy? Considering the continuation of racism and racist programs and policies that continue to be present as obstacles to black equality in America, that answer is no.

At the time of this writing, people are protesting the deaths of unarmed Black people by law enforcement officers, giving a continuation to the feeling that black life is still a devalued life in our society. Of course, some people are trying to say racism is not an issue in the killing of unarmed black people. There is a troubling pattern of video footage of unarmed black people being shot or killed by police. Compared to video footage where similarly situated white people who are armed and do resist the commands of the police are arrested and not shot or killed, the pattern indicates that there is a negative bias against black people by law enforcement. There is no indication that black people kill police officers at a higher rate than their counterparts, so a bias should not exist. Based on the percentage of black people killed in relationship to the number of white persons that are killed by law enforcement, there is an apparent bias. The killing of black people by the police is not centralized or localized but appears to happen throughout the United States, which seems to confirm that this is evidence of a systemic and institutionalized practice, or racism. And these killings are considered a continuation of the practices of lynching.

Let me be clear, I believe that the vast majority of police or peace officers are here to serve and protect the public. Law enforcement is an essential part of the fabric of our society and is necessary for the protection of our freedoms. This book is not about the police, but there is concern about the existence of a group of individuals who have the systemic and institutionalized power to act on their biases or bigotry without fear of being penalized for their actions.

But what about black police officers who kill unarmed black people? The courts have ruled that being of the same group as the victim does not create an automatic bar against racism. There is a term called internalized oppression or internalized racism that identifies the condition of a person of color who engages in the same racist acts towards their group as a white racist individual would.

Another example of stigmatization is the media's use of the terms thug and looters to describe anyone engaged in protest against systemic oppression. There is a difference between those who organize peaceful and lawful protest under the protections of the First Amendment to the United States Constitution and those who take advantage of a situation for their personal gain. The media often calls the peaceful protesters looters and thugs, thus stigmatizing the lawful assembly of those seeking legal remedies to unwarranted oppression against the black community. The media's use of the negative terms is an attempt to shame those who come to exercise their legal rights to lawful assembly and protest. Even Dr. King in his first march in Memphis experienced looters who were not part of the protest but who got the media's attention became part of an effort to shame the protest. Thus, the battle to stigmatize is just part of the effort to control the thinking of people for the purpose of racism's survival. We cannot allow the stigmatizing of words or programs or actions to be a stumbling block to progress.

Before and during the early days of the Civil Rights Movement being a jailbird had a tremendous stigma in the black community. Being a jailbird or going to jail was an immense embarrassment to the family and their good name. However, members of the Civil Rights Movement recognized that going to jail was an effective strategy to expose the injustice of inequality and segregation. They were able to overcome the stigma of going to jail, being called a jailbird, and the thought of being arrested and going to jail no longer had any negative power, but, in effect, became a badge of honor and courage. Let us do the same with the terms protester, victim, and Affirmative Action.

Chapter 7

THE VISION TO SEE

It's not what you look at that matters; it's what you see.

— HENRY DAVID THOREAU

RACISM IS A MATTER FOR WHITE PEOPLE TO END.

It took me a long time to accept and understand the notion that racism is a white person's problem. I believe that it was Don Benedict, who recruited me to be part of the Chicago Chapter of Clergy and Laity Concerned, whom I first heard utter those words. I was dismissive of that idea; I saw too many black people that racism harmed to believe that racism was the white person's problem.[18] If it was their problem what was their motivation to end it? I could hear the words of Dr. Martin Luther King regarding waiting and gradualism, and thought of the idea that black people would be given half a loaf of freedom and equality now and would have to buy the rest of their human and civil rights over an extended period. Based on the comfort of the dominant group

---

18   Joseph Barndt, *Dismantling Racism: The Continuing Challenge to White America*, Minneapolis, MN: Augsburg, 1991, viii-ix.

under the guise of the "narcotics of delay,"[19] I did not like that concept. But I would hear it from time to time, and I would hear my internal dissent as well.

It wasn't until I worked as an Affirmative Action Officer that I began to understand that racism is a white person's problem in much the same way alcohol is an alcoholic's problem. And unless white people are willing to get help to stop being racist the problem of white supremacy will remain. Thus, racism can't be fixed simply by legislation; it is an inherent and persistent evil that moves in the souls and hearts of those who enjoy the benefits. Nor can it be cured by simply holding out an olive branch. Like alcohol, racism is an insidious poison that brings destruction to the doers or abusers as well as to those with whom they interact. American racism exposes the hypocrisy of a system of democracy that proclaims justice and freedom while it continues to enjoy the fruits of the trees of enslavement, Jim Crowism, racism, injustice, bigotry, and hate.

One difficulty in seeing racism as the white community's problem is that there is not any visible pain for those who benefit from it, while the pains of the sufferers are evident. As with the alcoholic one can see the visible scars on the family that is at the mercy of this person. We read of the women caught in a domestic violence relationship with an alcoholic; we see the visible signs of the abuse. They are evidenced by black eyes, beatings, killings of these innocent people whose crime is loving and not leaving the abusive partner. We clearly see how the alcoholic is the victimizer and shudder at the thought of their actions. But it has not always been the case that our concern was for victims of alcoholics. We can remember a time when victims of domestic violence were told to return to the home and work it out. Others chose to not see it and just turned a blind eye and looked away. Too many times the victim was killed, and the killer was given treatment or not enough time locked away in prison. Racism has often been treated in the same manner –ignored.

---

19 Martin Luther King, Jr., *Why We Can't Wait,* New York, New York: Penguin Books, 1964, 128-129.

Racism is a disease, a cancer of the soul. It is inhumane to enslave, to kill, to deny another human being the right to enjoy life and to pursue their life's ambitions simply because of the color of their skin. We have a government that endorsed just such behavior and an institutionalized labor and wealth system that has benefitted and still benefits from the disparities of segregation and racism. So for racism to stop white people will have to stop being racists.

But what about people of color who are racist? In the book *The Possessive Investment in Whiteness* the author George Lipsitz states that people of color can and will support the systems of racism to the benefit of white supremacy for their individual purposes, but lack the systemic and institutionalized means to be racist against white people only against other people of color.[20]

One of the reasons that resistance to anti-racism continues is that it appears that black and white people can look at a situation and see it in two totally different ways. Having a difference of opinion is not racist by itself. However, it can be fuel for the continuation of a racist culture. Seeing things differently is not racist, but it could fuel racism. As Henry David Thoreau said, "It's not what you look at that matters; it's what you see."

For the past couple of decades I have worn glasses; glasses are an apparatus that improve my vision. My vision is affected by age, environment, and perhaps genetics; regardless of the causes, wearing glasses helps me to see. Glasses are a tool that affect my vision for the good; they help me to see what I need to see so that I can get to where I need to be.

Experience gives people a lens through which to view the world. Our experiences shape our vision and provide the lenses that we use to see the world in which we live. In America, black people have a different point of view based on their experiences or lenses. With that said, black people are not a monolith; all black people do not see eye to eye on all matters of race and racism.

---

20 George Lipsitz, *The Possessive Investment in Whiteness: How White People Profit from Identity Politics,* Philadelphia, PA: Temple University Press, 1998, viii.

However, there are some shared points of view regarding racism because of our shared collective experiences.

In the book, *Tragic Vision of the African American Religion,* Dr. Matthew Johnson discusses how tragic vision impacts one's ability to comprehend experience. He writes:

> The power of the tragic vision and perhaps its empowerment resides in its capacity to sustain sanity and the meaningfulness or value of experience while at the same time preserving a kind of radical objectivity or morally courageous realism. Tragedy and the Tragic Vision, as I understand them, grasp the integrity of human existence *as well as* its negation along with the facticity of their incongruity and hold them in delicate and dynamic tension.[21]

Racism is a horrible indictment of the American culture and society. The mere mention of racism causes a visceral reaction from black and white alike. Each group brings their experiences and understanding to mind whenever the term racism is heard. Being called a racist is hurtful to many white people, and they reject being labeled as such. They know that something is wrong with being called racist and seek to deflect its intentionality and pathos or pain.

Today there are attempts to deflect racism by trying to redefine who is racist and what racism is. The attempts are offered to imply that any form of dislike towards a white person by a person of color is racist or racism. These deflections are attempts to deal with the facticity of the incongruity that white people have been benefactors of racism. Thus, if a black mother does not want her son to date a white girl, that is called being racist. It is not racist; there is no evidence of systemic or institutional power or support behind the mother's efforts. The act may be biased; it may be mean, but it is not racist. Further to call it racist is simply an attempt to deflect attention away from confronting

---

21 Matthew V. Johnson, *The Tragic Vision of African American Religion,* New York, NY: Palgrave Macmillan, 2010, 26-27.

the historic reasons why a black mother may have such feelings as well as from reality that white people benefit from the system of racism. It is an attempt to escape a reality of privilege by creating a new definition of the actual problem.

Black people see the racism in the systems and institutions that engulf them; they see the enormity of the systemic influence of racism as it continues to play itself out in the world and America today. The pain and suffering that black people have endured have given black people a perspective, a lens born out of the tragedy of enslavement, Jim Crow, segregation, and the continuation of the disease of racism. Racism continues in many different ways, from closing schools in black neighborhoods, to increased incarceration, to degrading black women in the media. Bigotry and racism remain at the center of discriminatory behaviors that demean and devalue black people while providing comfort and support or privileges for white people.

There are white people who are well intended who can grasp the horrors of enslavement intellectually. There are some white people who consciously endeavor to understand the full impact of racism on our culture, society, the world, and people of color. They are the ones who historically have given their lives in support of freedom and equality for all people. In the 60s, they were among the Freedom Riders and other supporters of justice, whose blood also spilled on the landscape of hope as they gave the ultimate sacrifice to bring humanity back into harmony. While many white people can grasp the enduring problem of racism intellectually, many others cannot internalize how racism has continued to have lingering effects on communities of color and how white people have benefited from it directly or indirectly. They want to see equality where equality does not yet exist. Some hide behind a lack of exposure, refusing to hear the voices of those who have the experience that provides the ability to see racism. Thus, the truth of the larger society steeped in deniability is in effect a lie. The purpose of the deniability is to keep a sanity based on lies that run counter to the truth. They refuse the help needed to end racism and remain engulfed in a persistent yet implausible deniability.

The historical tragic vision provides the means to see better the existence of racism in our society. This vision exposes the sources of racism and how it continues to have a negative impact on our society. All things are not visible to the naked eye. Crime show after crime show has shown us where the forensic detectives will scour a crime scene often using a black light to expose residue and other stains not readily visible to the naked eye.

Those with this historical tragic vision can see where racism is visible and where it is not visible to the "naked" eye in our society. This vision serves as a black light exposing residue and stains on the fabric of America's freedom that are not visible to the naked eye of white supremacy and its supporters.

Thus, the pain from the tragic vision serves as the black light that allows some to have the vision to see what others can't see or won't see. Without the vision or experience, one can choose to not fully believe the horrors of the system of racism that continue to exist and persist. For a rational person, it is unfathomable to think that such planned and organized hate is doable and intentional and that such horror could still exist in the world today. Thus, the consciousness of the average person has to create a deniability to filter or cover the abuse that remains at the hands of racism. Otherwise, to accept the truth of racism as normative in our society is difficult, yet that is the reality. Racism is wrong, and in time the full truth will come to light that racism is still a daily part of American life.

Thus, the inability to admit past wrongs, the inability to see how one has benefitted from past injustices of racism, and the inability to see "I got there on my own" as a myth are all by-products of racism supported by the pedagogy and language of white supremacy. These are attempts to deflect the reality that racism is normative and that the vast majority of white people still benefit from its use and existence on a daily basis.

Chapter 8

THE TALK

Today I try to do well and be well with everyone I encounter.

— OPRAH WINFREY

There is a talk that every black parent has to give their children that "you are just as good as anyone else. And you will have to be twice as good to get half as much as your white counterparts." This talk helps to set an expectation that only through hard work can one expect to achieve in this world. This talk sets the expectation that no matter how much you may be taken for granted or told that you are not as good as someone else, you are just as good as they are, but life for you, the black child, it will be harder. But it appears that no matter how hard a person of color works there are still obstacles that serve to impede equality.

So, there is another talk that black parents or parents that have black children have to have with their children, especially their boys, and that is the talk about what to do when the police stop you.

Growing up in Chicago on the near Southside in an area called Kenwood-Oakland I had my unfair share of encounters of being stopped by the police.

Being a six-foot-tall teenager, I was possibly seen as a threat. I have seen videos, now that everyone carries a camera and with good reason, where people have been extremely defiant of the police. In the videos, people are demanding their rights, quoting case law and demanding that the police let them go. I am glad they were able to record their encounters and be in a position to share them with others. Police brutality is not new; it has been part of the American landscape for blacks since before the Fugitive Slave Laws of the 1700s. We have not always been treated kindly with these encounters. Being raised by relatives who were born in the late 1890s and early 1900s and who migrated to Chicago from Mississippi, I was told to have a respectful approach in my encounters with the police. In other words, always be polite to the officer; stand up straight; and look friendly. I didn't always succeed in looking friendly, but I was always respectful, agreeable and as non-threating as possible, even in my frustration with being stopped.

I remember a Chicago-cold December night just prior to Christmas Eve. I was running from the bus stop at 47th and Greenwood going to a friend's home to hang out before continuing home about three blocks away. As I was running and made it to Shakespeare School, by the flag pole, the police were coming down 46th Street, and when I saw them looking in my direction, I began to slow down. I am certain several people would today suggest don't slow down, (this was the 60s). They pulled over to where I had stopped and asked, "Where are you going?" I pointed, and they asked me why was I running? In a moment of pure impulse, but ever so politely, I gave the officer a look of amazement at the sincerity of the question, and simply responded, "Because it is cold out here." I didn't reply, "None of your business," or with some other smart remark, but simply a statement of logic and fact. They informed me that someone had been robbed or shot, and I expressed my concern for the victim.

The point is that even though the police officers may have approached me with some of the standard assumptions that black kids are up to no good, my demeanor was non-threating. It was as calm as someone could be who was approached by white officers on a cold night. I was able to dispel their saying I "looked like the suspect" by speaking to them, being respectful, and not bristling at the officers' audacity to approach me, just because I was running.

The talk that parents have with black children has changed somewhat. Children are now told to ask for a lawyer, not to submit to a search, and to say that your parents had instructed you to not say anything at any time to any police officer when stopped. The point is that parents have to give their black children, boys and girls a talk, on how they should behave when the police stop them. Even as an adult I am careful to carry some form of identification with me so that I can establish that I am not the person whom they may be seeking. Of course, we know that the talk has not worked for every single person.

But it is an important start because the response of respect sends a signal to the police officer that should elicit a gentler and professional response in return. When one responds with a "Yes officer, how may I help you?" or if one has a relaxed demeanor as if one is not afraid of this encounter, the officer may also be more relaxed. Many officers are conditioned to expect a hassle, and the non-confrontational mode is helpful.

Now, of course, there are some who will say "f" that; I'm a man or American; I can do what I want.[22] I am saying that discretion is more important that being defiant. Discretion will more often than not allow one to say "Thank you," and "Have a good night officer," versus being defiant that will often result in getting a night's stay with the officers or worse.

Consider using discretion by imaging this scenario: You have been sitting at a red light waiting for it to turn green, and when it does you notice a large truck that is about to run the light. As the person with the green light, you have every legal right to move through the intersection, but I believe you

---

22 There is now a debate arising concerning whether black persons stopped by the police should assert their rights and show defiance to law enforcement officers or engage in a practice of discretion in an effort to survive the encounter with law enforcement.

will allow discretion to take over and yield to the driver of the fast moving truck. Being able to encounter a police officer and move on is not about one's manhood or rights as an American; it is about survival. It is about being wise enough to know that going on your way, with a tip of the cap is better than being capped. This is the purpose of the talk black parents have with their children about the police. Save the confrontation for another time, if required. One doesn't have to forget the encounter; one can plan how to respond when the odds are more favorable. And on a cold winter night running down a street or being stopped by the side of a roadway, discretion may be one's only ally.

Let me simply say, try to create as comfortable an encounter as possible. I agree; you shouldn't have to do this. I understand the "ought to be" from what is the currently occurring reality of police encounters. I believe that discretion and documentation in this day and age are keys to a safer encounter with the police. There are plenty of good officers who believe in their oath to serve and protect, and that law enforcement is an honorable profession to provide for their families and serve their communities. The problem is that there are some officers out there who think and operate from a confrontational or siege perspective. Those are the ones who are problematic. Those are the ones that if you encounter one of them "the talk" may or may not make the difference.

The words here are only suggestions. Each parent of black children must decide for themselves how they will have the talk with their children and what parameters they want to set. There are plenty of resources on the internet, with local attorney offices, and others that offer additional advice on what to say when one is stopped by law enforcement. This chapter is not designed to be definitive or as a get out of trouble strategy. It is designed to start a conversation with white counterparts who have no idea that black parents have to have this talk with their children. It is clear that a fair percentage of white people, and some black people, believe that when a police officer approaches a black person, the black person has committed a crime, and that the police are justified in whatever action taken. We know that this is not always true. I just hope that this piece will open some minds that may have been closed.

Chapter 9

RESTORING THE HARMONY

*The world will not be destroyed by those who do evil, but
by those who watch them without doing anything.*

— ALBERT EINSTEIN

How do we restore the harmony with all humanity? That is a monumental task, yet it is doable, and we must try or we will all perish. To restore harmony, we will have to take another look at the discussion on trust in chapter three. To restore harmony, we will have to establish friendship contracts with those we encounter who are not like us. Thus, the restoration of harmony begins with each of us and those around us who are willing to live in harmony with each other. And given humanity's proclivity for greed and power, restoration of harmony will be a daunting task. Consider Jimi Hendrix's statement: "When the power of love overcomes the love of power the world will know peace." This statement serves as a North Star for us to move towards a true conversation about race that will bring about an end to racism. We need an aggressive push to spread the concept of love and respect to bring about the end of widespread bigotry. Friends live in a relationship of spreading or sharing concerns with one another. We must strive to make friends with people outside of our normal circle.

In Martin Marty's book *Friendship*, he posits that friendship requires freedom.[23] He writes that friendships are about risk. As adults, friendships often start when two strangers decide to take a chance encounter, interacting for only a moment, and finding in that moment an inkling, the germ of an idea, that this person whom I have never met before matters. From all the choices that one could have made that day, these two people decide that they will entertain the idea of friendship. In many cases, this is how you met your spouse, a chance encounter that turned into something more. Friendship is a mutual contract between parties involved. It is reciprocal in nature; it requires that all of the parties involved want to be in the relationship and that disagreements or disappointments will not break the bonds. In true friendships, the power of the friendship will create a salve that will ease pain, and create time and space for forgiveness and apology, enough space to keep the friendship intact.

For the most part, friendships developed after high school fit a pattern of demographic or ideological sameness, compatibility, or mutual benefit. Often we see ourselves reflected in the other person, and, thus, liking our reflection we decide that we like this version of ourselves, so we become friends. The freedom here is the freedom to choose from the herd. To choose inside the safe boundaries of conformity the homogeneous orthodoxy of the right background, the right education, the right religion, and the right elements to create an effective and stable merger of managed expectations.

But Marty also speaks of another type of friendship, a friendship based on the freedom to make a friend who is not like you, in essence, a heretical friendship. The homogenous orthodox friendship is no less valid than the heretical friendship. But homogenous orthodox friendship constrains the ability to break down barriers of bias and hinders the growth of the restoration of harmony outside of comfort zones.[24] Restorative harmony is hampered by friendships built on homogenous orthodoxy alone. Harmony is restored when people risk their stable expectations to be friends. By engaging in heretical

---

23 Martin E. Marty, *Friendship*, Texas: Argus Communications, 1980, 46.
24 Ibid., 52.

friendships, they are helping to break the entrenched bonds of bigotry. But too few are willing to risk comfort for the sake of a heretical friendship, especially when remaining in the elite status quo or comfort zone has its benefits.

Audre Lorde wrote, "The master's tools will never dismantle the master's house." This statement is on point.[25] White supremacy is an elite status of being; it pronounces white superiority over others. It creates and defends its positions with the master's tools of power, and propaganda or pedagogy, and cohesion. These tools are used to create a culture, in this case, white supremacy, that is dedicated to its existence and preservation at all costs.

I have witnessed people who engage in justice work establish an elite status group within the group. The elites within the group will protect their status by excluding people who think differently, who act differently, or who can't afford the dues. This is a form of violence, even though the violence is not physical as much as it is mental and emotional. Then the values and self-importance of the elite group are reinforced with their group speak of self-importance. As the group grows in size, there is often a cohesion and protection of the elite status group keeping them united and in control. So, no matter how much the group speaks about justice they are engaging in the same methodology or use of the master's tools. They are modeling the same process of creating a superior group over an inferior group and maintaining the elite status through methods that may be identified as the master's tools. These groups are not dismantling the master's house; they are merely reinforcing it. Unless people engage in heretical friendships and alliances they will not dismantle white supremacy or racism; they will do little more than reinforce the status quo.

Thus, the world needs more people who are willing to risk, to be vulnerable to exercise the freedom to make friends beyond their normal boundary. Ego, the need to be superior, is often the enemy of heretical friendships, as is

---

25 Audre Lorde, *Sister Outsider: Essays and Speeches,* Berkeley, CA: Crossing Press, 1984, 2007.

the fear of loss of status and stability. Friendship outside of the homogenous orthodoxy is hard when life can be so much easier staying within the boundary. For restorative harmony and the destruction of bigotry and racism, we need the movement that comes from moving outside of our comfort zones to form friendships.

Restorative harmony requires vulnerability on the parts of the principals involved, forgiveness on the parts of those who endure the lingering legacy of slavery and racism, and the removal of denial of the existence of white skin privilege and racism on behalf of white people. Black people will have to be able to move beyond the pain, and white people will have to stop acting like, pretending that they have gotten everything that they have on their individual merit. No one has succeeded without the help of others. Support for success has been provided. Some help has been individualized, some help has been systemic and institutionalized, and some help has been random, but all dreams and goals have been accomplished because somewhere along the line there was an outside help.

The restoration of harmony will only happen when trust between people develops and that trust becomes friendships outside of our comfort zones. We must be willing to be vulnerable, and willing to risk rejection from members of our existing groups. For an example of the courage for this, we may have to look at the turtle who advances when it is willing to stick its neck out.

CONCLUSION

We gain strength, and courage, and confidence by each experience...we must do that which we think we cannot.

— *ELEANOR ROOSEVELT*

Thank you for reading this book and not keeping your head in the sand of "If we don't discuss racism or race issues, they do not exist." Like the turtle, you are willing to stick your neck out because you have taken a great step towards addressing issues of bigotry and racism. By reading this book, you have gone further than most people in addressing this disease that continues to plague our nation and planet. I trust that the things that you have read will create within you a stirring to help to fix "things," to make a commitment to reform or change thinking that permits bigotry and racism to remain powerful agents of oppression in our society. I challenge you to have twelve conversations about race over the upcoming year. I further challenge you over the next twelve months to try to make twelve new friends or acquaintances who are outside of your normal circle of friends. None of us, because of the accident of birth or by our "race," is inherently or innately better than another person. Socialization, application of individual gifts, processes of nurture, and some systemic advantages have allowed some persons to prosper where others have failed or fallen short of their potential in life, but it doesn't make a person innately superior. What you are being asked to do is to stop racism from occurring and remaining entrenched at an institutionalized level, where groups of people are negatively affected based on skin color or some other inherent physical manifestation or trait.

Racism hurts all of us. Racism hurts us all in many untold but telling ways. We have witnessed where people of color who have been given the opportunity to advance have excelled. There are countless examples of people of color who, when given the chance, became leaders in their fields of human endeavor. Thus, as a society we know that skin color is not a bar to ability.

White supremacy and racism will end when white people stop being racist. And will decide to eradicate fully their desire to control and continue to benefit from the privileges that they receive from the racism in our culture. That does not mean that people of color are powerless in the battle against racism, but since racism is learned and starts in the heart, white people must have a change of heart for racism to end.

There is an Aesop fable about two frogs. One frog lived in a marsh with plenty of water and food, and another frog lived in a rut by the side of the road. The marsh frog tried to get the side of the road frog to move to the marsh where life was better and safer. But the side of the road frog refused; "he could not bring himself to move from the place to which he had become accustomed."[26]

White supremacy will remain as long as white people control the mechanisms of racism, the structures and infrastructures that allow systemic and institutionalized racism to persist. This position of power has been too difficult for them leave; it is a place to which they have become accustomed. Too

---

26 Aesop, *Aesop's Fables*, editor, George Stade, New York, NY: Barnes and Noble Classics, 2003, 147.

many white people are fearful that if they remove these barriers to progress and abandon this control that people of color will be as hostile to them as they have historically been to people of color. However, the evidence of the record shows that where black people have come to power, by and large, they have not engaged in any form of systemic revenge. There are exceptions, but the exception is not the rule. For the most part, the record shows cooperation and reconciliation as the normative practice for people of color in power.

Fear is a major factor that keeps white people from relinquishing their power. Friendship will help to remove that fear and establish a sense of trust that vulnerability will not be punished but honored. It will be hard, but to have restored harmony, we must try. Again, the record has demonstrated that where black and other people of color have exercised the power, they have not engaged in acts of retaliation, but instead in reconciliation leading to a restoration of harmony.

When racism is abolished from our society, then we as Americans will fully experience the unifying theory of the United States of America found in the Declaration of Independence (US 1776): "that all men [people] are created equal, that they are endowed by their Creator with certain unalienable Rights, that among these are Life, Liberty, and the pursuit of Happiness." Then we will have created a new reality consistent with a creation that is in harmony with itself.

Now that you have read this material and digested it I trust that you will see that notions of genetic superiority are not so. I trust that you will have all the success in life that you desire and in turn you take the responsibility to help others and not just those who look like you. This call to end bigotry is a call based in hope to all people, and not just one group, so that the world we live in can be a place of peace and harmony where "no bigotry allowed" rules our hearts.

Thank you for reading.

ABOUT THE AUTHOR

Ronald Bonner is a skilled and experienced speaker, facilitator, and workshop leader. He is the former Assistant to the President of the United Church of Christ for Affirmative Action and Equal Employment Opportunity in Cleveland, Ohio. In that role, he organized and led anti-racism and diversity workshops and had search committee oversight. During that time, he served on the Executive Board of Project Equality and worked on a project with the Department of Justice serving as the Train the Trainer facilitator. As the Manager of Multicultural Resources for Augsburg Fortress Publishers based in Minneapolis, Minnesota, he had the responsibility of increasing the portfolio of people of color of resources. His success in that role saw an increase in revenue for resources and several key new resources written by people of color authors. Currently, he is pastor of The Lutheran Church of the Atonement in Northwest Atlanta, Georgia.

Ronald is available for speaking and training engagements. To contact him, just visit his Facebook page at No Bigotry Allowed: Losing the Spirit of Fear.

ENDORSEMENTS

This jewel of a volume may just be the one that catapults many people into becoming anti-racist! Pastor Bonner has spent a great amount of time thinking through why strides to change racial justice in the church and society have not have a great impact. He undertakes an heroic effort to offer a small, yet powerful, volume on the issues that makes change so difficult. At the heart of the difficulty of addressing issues related to race, lies bigotry, according to Bonner. "Bigotry is the force that drives the effectiveness of institutionalized bias and systemic power that creates institutionalized injustice." And it is this predisposition to bigotry that prevents us from having meaningful conversations that might help to build relationships that transcend race. His examination of the phenomenon of race relations offers an historical overview of the development of race as a social construct in the 15th century through its present incarnation as "the New Jim Crow" and the #Blacklivesmatter movement. Bonner's approach offers a method for evaluating why and how race relations sometimes go so bad but also offers concrete suggestions for how they can, potentially, be saved. This approach would well be utilized internally by a congregation as well as externally, when congregational members interact with those in the workplace. I would suggest that all congregations of the ELCA purchase it for their church libraries and use them for some of their adult forums.

The Rev. Dr. Cheryl S. Pero, Director The Rev. Dr. Albert "Pete" Pero, Jr., Multicultural Center

Bonner's book arrives right on time. He names the issues, provides prophetic challenges, and shows that there is a balm in Gilead for the sin of racism. Bonner shows the necessary path of honest conversation, meaningful repentance, and serious commitment to transformative action that will allow us to grow in liberation and grace together. For those serious about issues of race this book is essential reading. If you want to live in courage, speak truth to power, confront racism effectively, and experience the Reign of God for all God's children let Bonner lead and guide you.

The Rev. Dr. Mark Francisco Bozzuti-Jones Priest for Pastoral Care and Community, award winning author and author of the Gospel of Barack Hussein Obama according to Mark and the Rastafari Book of Common Prayer.

Made in the USA
Coppell, TX
21 June 2020

29047433R00046